Feng Shui

FOR THE GARDEN

A PRACTICAL AND EASY TO USE GUIDE TO THE ART OF FENG SHUI IN THE GARDEN

Jonathan Dee

Published in the United Kingdom in 2000 by Caxton Editions
20 Bloomsbury Street
London WC1B 3QA
a member of the Caxton Publishing Group

Designed and Produced for Caxton Editions by Open Door Limited
80 High Street, Colsterworth, Lincolnshire, NG33 5JA
Illustration: Andrew Shepherd, Art Angle
Colour separation: GA Graphics Stamford

Title: Feng Shui, For the Garden
ISBN: 1-84067-238-2

Picture credits

PhotoDisc images: 1, 4, 6, 7, 8, 12, 14, 18, 20, 24, 26, 32, 34, 36, 38, 46, 48, 50, 52, 54, 56, 59, 60, 62, 63, 64, 65, 66, 69, 70, 72, 74, 75, 76, 78, 80, 84, 85, 86, 87, 89, 92, 94

Elizabeth Whiting Associates: 13, 14, 58, 66, 71, 72, 81, 84, 89

Clive Nichols Photography: 1, 8, 59, 60, 61, 62, 63, 64, 73, 77, 79, 82-83, 88, 91, 93

Feng Shui

FOR THE GARDEN

Jonathan Dee

CAXTON EDITIONS

Contents

Contents

Introduction

The ancient Chinese art of Feng Shui exists to create a harmonious environment in tune with the forces of nature. It could be thought of as the earliest "green" philosophy. The name literally means "wind and water" because like the breeze or the meandering stream the energies of heaven and the earth should flow gently through our lives, our homes, and more to the point of this book, our gardens.

The Chinese sages who thought up the art of Feng Shui were convinced that its correct usage would promote health, happiness and a sense of well being with the world. However the practice of Feng Shui is not some faintly remembered superstition left over from the days of the emperors. On the contrary, it is a living art form which has now spread all over the world bringing spiritual and practical benefits to those who are fortunate enough to live in such a harmonious environment. Apart from the more mystical viewpoint, good Feng Shui is also good design.

There is an opinion that a Feng Shui garden must necessarily be an oriental garden but this is not so. If you have the calm Zen gardens of Japan in mind then think again. Though these gardens embody a practice similar to Feng Shui, they are intended to encourage a meditative state using calm water features, shade, and patterns in gravel and stones. Often Zen gardens are totally devoid of plant life. In Feng Shui terms a space like this would be described as Yin whereas in the West our gardens, often bursting with vitality are on the Yang side (see p.16) as indeed are our busy lives.

It is because we are so busy that Feng Shui should make a contribution to our lives. In this highly technological world it is easy to forget that we are all children of nature and that our relationship with the world is essential to our sense of spirituality. Feng Shui seeks to harmonise our existence with the world of nature. It may seem superfluous to point it out, but we are profoundly affected by the environment and our surroundings can help to heal our spirits or to harm them. Feng Shui can be seen as the opposite to "Sick building syndrome" where the surroundings actively make the unfortunates who live or work there are more aggressive, prone to anxiety and illness. Lets make sure that our gardens, which should be havens of peace and pleasure serve to enhance our lives not to blight them.

How to Begin

To apply the principles of Feng Shui to the garden it is vital that we get the basics right. There are several stages to go through and understand before we start to move things about or rearrange them in your personal space.

Mapping your garden.

The first thing to do is to equip yourself with a tape measure, a compass and several sheets of graph paper because you will need to measure your garden accurately and draw a plan of the space that you wish to harmonise the Feng Shui way. After you have completed your plan find the centre of your garden by drawing diagonal lines from corner to corner. Don't worry if your garden is an irregular shape, just "square it off" by filling in the missing portions with a dotted line. Now you have found the centre go there and stand in the middle of your garden and use a compass to find the cardinal points of North, South, East and West. Once you have discovered these mark them boldly on your plan. Now find the intermediate points of Northeast, Southeast, Southwest and Northwest and note their positions as well. You have now completed the first stage and discovered the areas governed by the Eight Directional Trigrams (see p. 29).

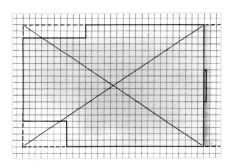

The surrounding landscape

Still standing in the middle of your garden take a good look at the surrounding landscape. For many of us this will provide a view of roofs which for the purposes of Feng Shui should be regarded as hills. The ideal situation for your property is one in which your house and garden are partially enclosed in a sort of "horseshoe formation" either by natural features or by surrounding buildings.

However if the slopes behind your house are particularly steep then the Chi, like a swift torrent will sweep down into your property very fast and measures must be taken to slow down its passage. Meandering paths and barriers of fences or plants are the usual way to accomplish this.

Negative influences

Remember that Chi will enter your garden from all directions and that it will bring some of the influences it passes through to your garden. So take note of any industrial estates with large, overhanging structures such as cranes or places associated with death such as cemeteries in your area. The impact of large structures that are visible from your property should be lessened by the softening effects of shrubbery or trees, which should ideally screen the offending structure from view. If the Chi that enters your garden pass through a cemetery this is not necessarily unfortunate. This Chi is generally harmless if the cemetery is to the North of your property. If it lies in any other direction then some sort of screening technique will be required to encourage this negative Chi to pass around your property rather than through it. Notably ugly buildings or sharp corners directed towards your garden should also be screened off if at all possible.

Having taken into account the geographical layout of the surrounding area it is now time to consider the influences of the Symbolic Animals of the four cardinal directions, each of which bring a particular type of Chi into your property (see p. 15).

Try to lessen the impact of large structures visible from your garden by softening the effect with shrubs and trees.

12

Ugly buildings and sharp corners should be screened off or disguised in some way to lessen their negative influence.

The facing direction

In terms of garden Feng Shui the topic of the Facing Direction causes the most controversy. In short, it is the question "Which way does your garden face?" In this book we will return to this subject again and again, but in essence when you stand in the centre of your garden which way do you tend to face? If the answer is that you don't favour any particular direction then the answer to this difficult query is probably the way by which you entered the garden. Assuming that you are attempting to assess an enclosed rear garden then facing direction will probably be the back door of your house.

The facing direction is important because it governs the predominant type of Chi that enters and influences your property. It is dealt with more fully on p.15.

The facing direction of your garden is determined simply by the direction you prefer to face when you are standing in it.

The Principles

To master the art of Feng Shui it is necessary to become familiar with some new concepts. These include "The Breath of Life", the Polarities of Yang and Yin, the nature of the Five Elements and the influence of the Elemental Directions. Fortunately these are not difficult to understand so we'll begin with the cosmic animating principle known as Chi.

Sheng Chi and Sha Chi

Oriental tradition holds that the universe is filled with an energy called Chi (pronounced Kee), otherwise known as Qi or Ki. This force is considered to be the vital energy which animates everything. This concept has no direct parallel in western thought, the nearest being a sort of cosmic principle like the Christian doctrine of the Holy Spirit. However for our purposes it may be easier of think of Chi as the breath of life itself. This "universal breath" flows through us and around us creating our vitality and energising the luck potential of our surroundings. This free flowing Chi is thought to be harmonious and auspicious and is more correctly known as Sheng Chi. This form of Chi moves in sinuous curved lines, flowing in a fashion exactly like water or gentle breezes. This is the reason that oriental gardens rarely include straight lines in their design and that sharp corners and threatening natural features are considered to be harbingers of bad luck.

If, however the free passage of the benevolent energy of Sheng Chi is blocked or disrupted in some way then its luck bearing potential is spoiled and it becomes Sha Chi which collects and stagnates bringing misfortune in its wake. Sha Chi is extremely destructive and can cause depression, ill feeling within a family, the loss of prosperity and bad health. It is important to remember that Sha Chi is said to move in straight lines and strike at the family fortunes like a "secret arrow". Much of practical Feng Shui is concerned with transforming the negative Sha Chi into its more beneficial counterpart and minimising the chances of Sha Chi overwhelming one's garden or living space.

The polarities

Both types of Chi are made up of opposite yet complementary qualities. These are known as Yang and Yin. This concept derives from the ancient Chinese religion of Taoism (pronounced Dow-ism). The Tao means "The Way" and is thought to be the source of everything that exists. The Tao is divided into both positive and negative components and these are of course, Yang and Yin. Sheng Chi is energised by its constant motion between one and the other. Therefore maintaining a balance between Yang and Yin is important to foster good luck.

    Yang is the active component of Chi. Its nature is bright, upwardly moving, masculine and active. Yin, on the other hand, is dark, tending downwards, feminine and passive. However, it is definitely not the case that Yang is "good" and Yin "bad". The two ideally co-exist in perfect balance. Think of them like the opposite poles of a magnet. Yin would be the principle of attraction because it is passive and Yang would be the principle of repulsion because it is active. One may think of these polarities as night and day, hot and cold, summer and winter.

The ancient Chinese sages who devised this form of mysticism even went so far as to suggest that both Yang and Yin were so inextricably linked that they each contain the seed of the other. So in the well known Tai Chi symbol there is a small circle of light within the dark area and a circle of darkness within the light.

Yang and Yin only exist in reference to each other, that which is not Yin must by nature be Yang and vice versa. Below are listed some of the complementary pairs of opposites which are associated with the concept of Yang and Yin. However, by necessity this must be a partial list only, it could conceivably be extended to include every pair of opposites that exist in the universe.

Yang	Yin
Male	Female
Light	Dark
Hot	Cold
Light	Heavy
Hard	Soft
Positive	Negative
Heaven	Earth
Fire	Water
Mountain	Valley
Sharp	Blunt
Right	Left
Up	Down
Front	Back
Spirit	Body
Solid	Hollow
Angular	Curved
Odd Numbers	Even Numbers
Moving	Static
Day	Night
Sun	Moon

Feng Shui is concerned with maintaining a perfect balance between Yang and Yin so that the beneficial Sheng Chi, which is the combination of both can flow freely through our lives. When we are happy and comfortable in our surroundings Yang and Yin are considered to be in harmony, it is therefore extremely desirable for these principles to be balanced especially in the garden.

The Five Elements

In the traditions of western mysticism there are said to be four Elements: Earth, Water, Air and Fire which express the states of matter, solid, liquid, gaseous and pure energy. At one time everything was thought to be made of combinations of these four elements. In China however, the ancient Taoist masters favoured a system of five Elements that they called Wu-Xing. Unlike their western equivalents, these Elements do not symbolise what things are made of but they do represent a sequence of changes, a sort of evolution from one state of being to another.

The Five Elements are:

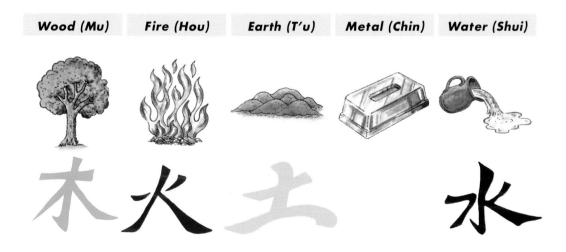

Wood (Mu)   **Fire (Hou)**   **Earth (T'u)**   **Metal (Chin)**   **Water (Shui)**

Taken in this order the Elements make up the "Creation Cycle" as follows:

Wood fuels Fire.

Fire creates Earth (in the form of ash).

Earth creates Metal.

Metal can flow like Water.

Water feeds Wood.

This is the harmonious arrangement of the Elements, however, if this cycle is not maintained and the elements appear out of sequence then the "Cycle of Destruction" comes into play.

Wood exhausts Earth	Earth pollutes Water	Water douses Fire	Fire melts Metal	Metal cuts Wood

The cycles of creation and destruction become more important when we consider that each of the Elements is associated with a direction of the compass. Therefore certain areas of your garden and indeed your home will be connected to an Element. The objects, physical features and use of these areas can therefore be in tune with the element of that direction or cause complications because they are the wrong colour, sited unsuitably or made of the wrong material. An understanding of the symbolic correspondences of the Five Elements is vital to achieve the true harmony of Feng Shui in your garden. For instance, the direction allocated to the Fire Element is the South, therefore it is obvious that placing a pool or some other water feature in this area of the garden would not be harmonious because according to the "Destruction Cycle" Fire douses Water. Thus good fortune from the South will be spoiled by the inclusion of the Water element in this area. If however, a brick barbecue is sited in the South then this combination of "earthy" brickwork to make such a fiery item in the Fire area would do much to improve your fortunes because according to the "Creation Cycle" Fire creates Earth. On the other hand, if your barbecue was made of metal then we're back to the Destruction Cycle because Fire melts Metal.

The directions that are associated with each Element are as follows:

> *Wood corresponds to the East and the South-east.*
>
> *Fire corresponds to the South.*
>
> *Earth corresponds the Centre and also to the North-east and South-west.*
>
> *Metal corresponds to the West.*
>
> *Water corresponds to the North.*

The cardinal directions of East, South, West and North are the most important of these and will be dealt with separately under "The Symbolic Animals" (p.26).

Of course if you do have a pool in the Fire direction all is not lost. There are ways of turning the Destructive Cycle into its more harmonious counterpart. Water and Fire are in conflict because there is no Wood (Water feeds Wood, Wood fuels Fire) so the addition of a wooden trellis or some other prominent feature made of this Element would cure the problem. The same goes for any conflict between Elements. The reason that Elements are in conflict is that there is a factor missing so any problem between Fire and Water can be cured with Wood, similarly, a conflict between Metal and Wood can be cured by the addition of Water. Here is a table of possible elemental conflicts and their associated elemental cures.

Conflict	Cure
If Wood conflicts with Metal (Metal cuts Wood)	add Water
If Water conflicts with Fire (Water douses Fire)	add Wood
If Earth conflicts with Water (Earth pollutes Water)	add Metal
If Fire conflicts with Metal (Fire melts Metal)	add Earth
If Wood conflicts with Earth (Wood exhausts Earth)	add Fire

Apart from being allocated specific directions, the five Elements also have a series of symbolic correspondences such as shapes, colours and images associated with them. These correspondences will help to harmonise an otherwise troublesome area.

Element	Directions	Colour	Shapes
Wood	East, South-east	Green, light blue	Rectangle
Fire	South	Red	Triangle
Earth	Centre, North-east, South-west	Yellow	Square
Metal	West, North-west	White, metallic tints	Circle, Oval
Water	North	Black, dark blue	Wavy lines

So if a conflict between Wood and Earth has occurred one need not literally light a bonfire to add the missing Fire element. Something that is triangular in shape such as a small fir-tree, or a red coloured object would do just as well to symbolise the Fire Element. Similarly, if the conflict exists between Earth and Water then the solution would be to add an item which is white in colour or in the shape of a circle or oval to symbolise the Metal Element to defuse the problem.

The Symbolic Animals

Before we move on to a more detailed analysis of the eight areas of the garden we should pause to take a look at the cardinal directions of North, South, East and West and their associated animal symbols.

Each of the animal symbols represent a certain type of energy that flows into the garden carrying the nature of the direction from which it has come. An important feature of Garden Feng Shui is the direction the garden "faces". In many ways' the symbolic animal of that direction will set the tone for the entire garden.

It is important to remember that the influences of any of these "flavours" of Chi entering your personal space can be complicated by features in the surrounding area. A cemetery in the immediate locality could be the most troubling influence unless it lies in the North, the direction of the Black Turtle.

The North

The Northerly direction is symbolised by the Black Turtle. Just as its symbol implies, energy arriving from the North tends to be slow moving and rather sleepy. It is, however as protective to your garden as the shell is to the turtle. The Black colouring of the animal refers to the Water Element, North being its associated direction. The nature of this type of energy is Yin, and though it is a calming influence too much of it would be depressive and gloomy within your garden.

The South

The Red Bird, also known as the Phoenix is the symbolic animal of the South. Its fiery nature is expressed as the heat of summer. This is the most Yang of the animal symbols and energy arriving from the South will be warm, energetic, optimistic and fortunate. However, it is important to remember that good Feng Shui in the garden relies on a harmonious mixture of Yang and Yin so too much heat energy flowing from the South would be a bad thing somewhat analogous to creating a desert.

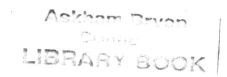

The East

The East is the direction of that most oriental of beasts the Dragon. Its colour is green to indicate the Element Wood. It also has an association with the growth of new shoots so this area is considered to be extremely fertile and benevolent. Because this is the direction of the sunrise and of the season of Spring, the energy that arrives from the Green Dragon is innovative and fertile. In many ways the area of the Dragon can be considered to be a balance between the calm energies of the Northern Turtle and the exuberant Southern Bird.

The West

In contrast to the new life symbolised by the Green Dragon, the West is represented by the dangerous White Tiger. This fearsome beast presides over the area of sunset and is also associated with the autumnal season, so just as the Dragon governs new growth, the White Tiger indicates decrease and decay. Energies from the Westerly direction are stormy and disruptive and if left unchecked can cause havoc both within your garden and in your life. Generally barriers are placed in this area to prevent the White Tiger from roaming freely through your property. However, if your garden "Faces" the sleepy North, then a shot of wild Tiger energy might just be what your garden needs to inject some vitality into your life.

The Eight Directional Trigrams

As we have seen the concept of direction is very important in Feng Shui generally, and absolutely vital when one attempts to plan a garden according to these ancient principles.

People who are familiar with indoor Feng Shui will also be familiar with the Pa Kua mirror which is usually placed on the front door or in a window adjacent to the door to deflect "secret arrows" which might harm the fortunes of those living within the dwelling. This mirror is eight sided, each of its segments contains a figure of three lines called a trigram which are derived from the Chinese book of oracles, the I Ching.

A Pa Kua mirror - used to deflect "secret arrows" away from a dwelling.

The trigrams on the mirror are arranged in a sequence called "The Early Heaven Arrangement" which is said to be passive in nature, so the arrangement around the mirror would correctly be called the Yin Pa Kua. Thus it is capable of deflecting disruptive or harmful Yang energy. However in planning the perfect garden another arrangement of trigrams need to be borne in mind. This is the Yang Pa Kua which is very similar to its domestic equivalent except that the trigrams will be arranged in the "Later Heaven Sequence".

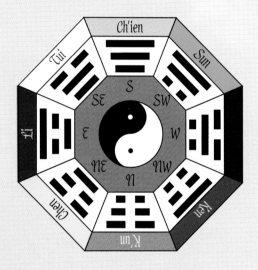 

The Yin Pa Kua of the "Early Heaven Arrangement".

The Yang Pa Kua of the "Later Heaven Sequence".

The Yang Pa Kua allocates each of the eight areas to a point of the compass starting in the South with the Trigram Li, which is associated with the Fire Element and the Red Phoenix.

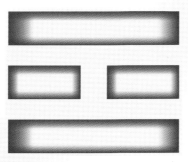

Since the South is the direction of the Fire element, the trigram Li represents a flame.
Li symbolises illumination, inspiration, clarity of mind and knowledge. Since heat is a
feature of the symbol, the season associated with it is the height of Summer. The
family member that Li most closely relates to the Middle daughter who is
considered to be both beautiful and intelligent. The trigram is said
to influence the wellbeing of the eyes, the heart and the
circulation of the blood. Creatures associated with the trigram
include the pheasant, probably derived from the Red Phoenix of the South, the turtle
and the goldfish. The symbolic colour of the southern sector of the garden is orange,
its plants are those which thrive in heat such as tomatoes or indeed those which
possess heat such as peppers and chillies. Traditional thinking states that
trees in this area should be somewhat dried out, and
the usual Feng Shui bar on dead plants does not
seem to apply to the area of Li.

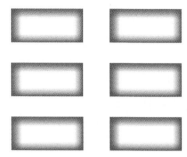

The Trigram K'un is placed in the Southwest

The literal translation of K'un is "Earth" in the sense of Mother Earth, and indeed this trigram signifies many maternal associations in its symbolism. As might be expected the family member that it signifies is the mother, and since in ancient Chinese tradition it was the mother's duty to feed her family, the trigram came to represent the stomach and the abdomen. The idea of motherhood inherent in K'un ensures that the trigram also symbolises the womb.

The nature of the trigram is receptive, its colours are generally dark hued or black. The symbolic animals of K'un are the Ox, the mare, the cow and the industrious ant. The season with which K'un is associated is the Late Summer, the time of harvest.

K'un is also associated with root vegetables such as potatoes, swedes and carrots, and also with bulbs which could be regarded as a sort of symbolic womb allowing new growth to develop in darkness. The Southwest area of the garden is said to relate directly to the mother or other maternal figures expressing the health and fortunes of the lady of the house.

The Trigram Tui is placed in the West

The gentle Tui symbolises the Youngest Daughter. Its name means "The Lake" it is associated with the depths of the psyche, with healing and magic. The nature of the trigram is joyful and rather sensual. The colours of this area are traditionally those of the setting sun or the russets and reds of falling leaves, therefore the symbolic season of Tui is the Autumn. The animals associated with the trigram are sheep, birds and the graceful antelope. The wellbeing of the mouth and lips are traditionally associated with Tui. In terms of the garden the Western sector would be an ideal location for magnolias and gardenias. Since the West corresponds to the element Metal which is compatible with the watery nature of Tui the Lake , the trees associated with this direction tend to like a great deal of moisture therefore Mangroves and trees that habitually grow by the shores of the sea or lakes are recommended.

The name of the trigram Ch'ien means "Heaven" and its direction is the North West. It is associated with the father or the head of the family. The parts of the body that symbolically connect with the figure are the head, especially the skull and by the extension of this idea, the mind itself comes under the auspices of Ch'ien.

The nature of the trigram is strong and creative, its colours are white and gold, and its symbolic animals are the horse, the lion and the tiger. The season with which Ch'ien is linked is the Late Autumn.

In terms of the garden, the Ch'ien area directly relates to the health and fortunes of the head of the household. It is a suitable place to plant fruit trees if space allows or perhaps chrysanthemums. It is also considered an auspicious site for a herb garden.

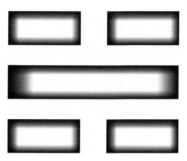

The Trigram K'an represents the North

K'an is translated as "Water" and ideally occurs in the Watery direction, the North. In Chinese tradition the North is considered to be the area of danger because throughout the history of that great nation calamities such as barbarian invasions, devastating storms and plagues all seemed to sweep down on the people from that direction. In many ways the Chinese considered this trigram to represent water in its frozen state so it is probably more accurate to think of it as representing ice. Thus, K'an is associated with the season of Winter, its nature is considered to be cunning, perilous and as treacherous as black ice. Its colours are black and dark blue and its symbolic animals are the rat and the pig. The family member associated with the trigram is the Middle Son who may have been envious of his older brother Chen.

It is obvious that this area of the garden must be treated with caution because of the potential of disharmony coming from the North. However this is a good place for a mobile water feature to create much needed chi in this essentially stagnant area. The plants associated with K'an also tend to be aquatic so a water feature here would be a necessity for growing reeds, bulrushes and water lilies. The symbolic tree of the trigram is that most oriental type, the willow though the alder is also said to have an association with K'an.

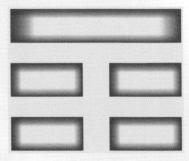

The name of the trigram Ken means "Mountain" so a symbolic mound of some kind would be a good idea in the North-eastern sector of the garden. Since the symbolic plants of this trigram are alpine flowers and heathers this would be an ideal place for a rockery. This is especially the case since the symbolic colour of Ken is violet and many alpine plants have a purplish tinge. If a rockery in the north-eastern sector of the garden is out of the question then you really do need something that will rise high like a mountain. Traditional Feng Shui thinking would hope for a gnarled old tree in this area. Obviously one cannot plant an old tree so a plant that yields nuts, or an olive tree would be an equally good idea.

The nature of a mountain is stillness. Great mountain ranges like the Himalayas are considered to be the backbone of the world just as the Pennine range is often called "the backbone of England" and as the Rockies are "the backbone of America". Thus, Ken is associated with the spine, and since its symbolic family member is the dextrous Youngest Son the hands are also thought to be influenced by this trigram. The symbolic animals of Ken are the dog, the leopard, the bull and the mouse.

The Trigram Chen symbolises the East

The name of the trigram means "Thunder". It is associated with regeneration because a downpour in a thunderstorm renews the fertility of the earth. However the nature of the trigram is volatile because of the damage that lightning and sudden floods can cause. The family member that the trigram Chen symbolises is the eldest son, the heir to the household. The parts of the body associated with this symbol are the feet and also the throat and thus the voice. Its season is Spring when all of life is gaining strength. The associated colour of the trigram is yellow and its symbolic animals are the dragon, the eagle and the swallow.

In terms of the garden the eastern segment is a particularly good place for flower beds or for evergreen trees. In many oriental gardens this area is reserved for the cultivation of bamboo.

The Trigram Sun represents the Southeast

There are two possible interpretations of the name Sun. It can either represent wind or the element Wood. By nature this trigram is like a gentle breeze or an early shoot. It is gentle and adaptable and is associated with the dutiful Eldest Daughter of a traditional Chinese family. The Eldest daughter is connected with the concepts of endurance, quiet determination and fair play. The season associated with the trigram is Early Summer and the body parts that is said to influence are the thighs, the upper arms, the lungs and the nervous system. The symbolic animals of the trigram are the rooster, the snake and the tiger.

The symbolic colour associated with Sun is green so the south-easterly segment of the garden is the perfect place for a lawn, though both poppies and lilies would also be auspicious in this area. However, if these options don't suit your taste any tall trees in the sector governed by the gentle Sun would also be acceptable in Feng Shui terms.

Which Way Does Your Garden Face?

The next step is to find out how these eight trigrams relate to the fortunes of you and your family. For this we need to know which way you garden faces. Before we go on it should be pointed out that much of Feng Shui is intuitive so I suggest that you go and stand in the middle of your garden and have a good look at its surroundings. If you are blessed with a particularly splendid view then that will be the natural facing direction of the garden. If, on the other hand you find yourself in a fairly small, enclosed space with no obvious start point then you must count the way you entered the garden as the facing direction. In most cases this will be the back door of your dwelling. In gardens with more than one entrance you will have to use your best judgement as to which is used more regularly or seems to be the more important. Remember it is your garden and your feelings about it must be paramount so if you don't think that the back door is the starting point for your garden you will be right even if you consider it to begin at your dustbin a side door or even a shed. Only your feelings and intuition count on this subject.

The diagrams

Since you have already worked out the eight directions of the Yang Pa Kua and found where the trigrams sit in your garden space it is time to add another set of guidelines which should clarify things further. There are two ways of doing this. The first involves a diagram called the Lo Shu or "Magic Square" which is also used in interior Feng Shui, the second is somewhat easier in terms of the garden because you will have already made the eight necessary divisions by working out the directions of the trigrams. If you really want to be complicated you can use both to ensure that the Feng Shui of your personal space is completely and utterly harmonious. However, in practice if you get one system right the other will fall into line automatically. Why not experiment with both to find out which one fits into your personal space best?

The Lo Shu Magic Square method

The Magic Square is a diagram made up of nine squares in a 3 x 3 grid pattern. Each one of the squares is allocated a number and the Lo Shu is considered magical partly because even though there are eight possible ways to add the numbers together the answer will always be 15.

This diagram can be used in many ways such as in certain forms of Chinese astrology, but in this case we will content ourselves with dealing with the arrangement of space. All we have to do is to superimpose the diagram onto the plan of your garden thereby subdividing it into nine distinct areas. If you have any experience of Feng Shui within your home this process will already be familiar to you.

Using the Lo Shu in an open space will be easier if your garden is square or rectangular because you can elongate the Lo Shu to fit it. If however your garden is an irregular shape simply "square it off" and fill in any missing sections with a dotted line. Take special note of any area that does fall outside the garden boundaries because this will represent some factor that is missing or troublesome in your life and will need some Feng Shui rectification.

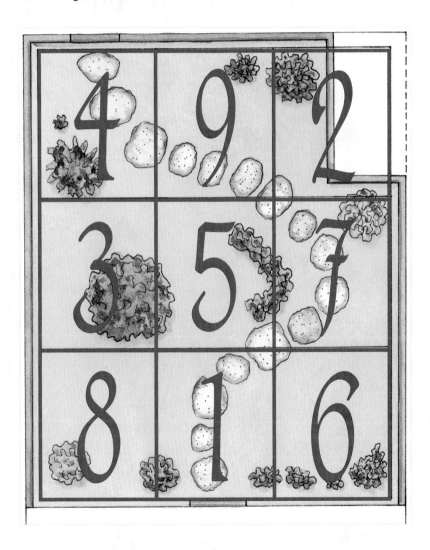

Assuming that we are dealing with a back garden, the entrance to the garden (or the facing direction) will occur in areas 8, 1 or 6. The furthest point away from the entrance will therefore be in areas 4, 9 or 2. Putting it another way, if you stand in the centre of the garden facing the back wall of your house or the direction which you have chosen that the garden faces you will be in area 5. To your left is area 7, and to your right is area 3. Area 1 is directly before you and area 9 directly behind. The other squares will fill in the gaps. This is known as the Eight Point Method.

Each area has a distinct set of associations which are used in conjunction with the meanings of the eight Trigrams to give a fuller picture of what each segment of the garden represents to you.

Square 1. (Front centre)

This area represents career ambition and status. It has a bearing on business dealings your personal potentials and the contribution you make to society.

4	9	2
3	5	7
8	**1**	6

Square 2. (Rear right)

Your relationships are symbolised by this sector. Romance especially is found here. Marriage and other types of long term partnerships too may be represented in this area.

4	9	**2**
3	5	7
8	1	6

Square 3. (Middle left)

This area refers to the past and was considered one of the most important by the ancient Chinese sages, who after all were ancestor worshippers. Your background, family relationships through the generations and your prospects of inheritance are symbolised in this area.

4	9	2
3	5	7
8	1	6

Square 4. (Rear left)

This is the sector of wealth dealing with your prospects of gaining and keeping hold of financial good fortune.

4	9	2
3	5	7
8	1	6

Square 5. (Centre)

Your health and physical well being are represented at the very centre of the garden. Keeping this area tidy is vital if you and your family are to remain hale and hearty.

4	9	2
3	5	7
8	1	6

Square 6. (Front right)

In Chinese tradition this is the area devoted to the gods and spirits. It also governs helpful allies of all sorts and people who will go out of their way to aid you.

4	9	2
3	5	7
8	1	6

Square 7. (Middle right)

This sector governs fertility, children and personal creativity. It also has a bearing on your talents, hobbies and the use of leisure time.

4	9	2
3	5	7
8	1	6

Square 8. (Front left)

This area refers to your education and knowledge and may regulate how open you are to new ideas and challenges to your preconceptions.

4	9	2
3	5	7
8	1	6

Square 9. (Rear centre)

The last square is the area of fame. This sector governs your reputation and the way that you are perceived by others. The Chinese regard this area as very important because honour and respect are intrinsic aspects of their culture.

4	**9**	2
3	5	7
8	1	6

Example 1.

If a garden has its entrance in the West, the area of the Trigram Tui, The Lake it will open into areas 8, 1 or 6. If we assume that the entrance is in the middle of a wall the relevant area will be 1. We can now consider the other areas and trigrams together, Ch'ien will occupy area 8, K'an will be found in area 3, Ken in area 4 and so on. The predominant energy flowing into this garden is from the potentially disruptive White Tiger of the West which immediately effects the career prospects (area 1). The stormy nature of the West can be muted by the addition of some of the plants associated with Tui such as a magnolia or even a still water feature (Tui means "Lake") such as a bird bath just inside the entrance (preferably to the left of the entrance see p.68) .

Area 1	**– Career is in the West corresponding to Tui.**
Area 8	**– Knowledge is in the Northwest corresponding to Ch'ien.**
Area 3	**– Ancestors is in the North corresponding to K'an.**
Area 4	**– Wealth is in the Northeast corresponding to Ken.**
Area 9	**– Fame is in the East corresponding to Chen.**
Area 2	**– Relationships is in the Southeast corresponding to Sun.**
Area 7	**– Children is in the South corresponding to Li.**
Area 6	**– Allies is in the Southwest corresponding to K'un.**
Area 5	**– Health lies at the centre of the garden and is associated with the Earth Element.**

NE

E

SE

N

S

NW

W

SW

Example 2.

If the garden entrance located towards the left hand corner of a wall in the South the "Palace of the Red Bird" the same system applies. In this case, the entrance is located in area 8 which is related to education and knowledge. The optimistic and intelligent influence of the trigram Li the flame is perfectly in tune with this sector and can be further enhanced by planting red or orange coloured flowers here. Likewise, proceeding clockwise into the area of the next trigram K'un which occupies sector 3 a rockery or even a small arrangement of pebbles would enhance the earthy nature of the trigram. Thus area 3 which relates to family background and ancestors would help maintain the well being of both one's mother and that of the lady of the house.

Area 1	**– Career is in the South corresponding to Li.**
Area 8	**– Knowledge is in the Southwest corresponding to K'un.**
Area 3	**– Ancestors is in the West corresponding to Tui.**
Area 4	**– Wealth is in the Northwest corresponding to Ch'ien.**
Area 9	**– Fame is in the North corresponding to K'an.**
Area 2	**– Relationships is in the Northeast corresponding to Ken.**
Area 7	**– Children is in the East corresponding to Chen.**
Area 6	**– Allies is in the Southeast corresponding to Sun.**
Area 5	**– Health lies at the centre of the garden and is always. associated with the Earth Element.**

Now try out the method in your garden. Remember to first allocate the trigrams to their respective directions.

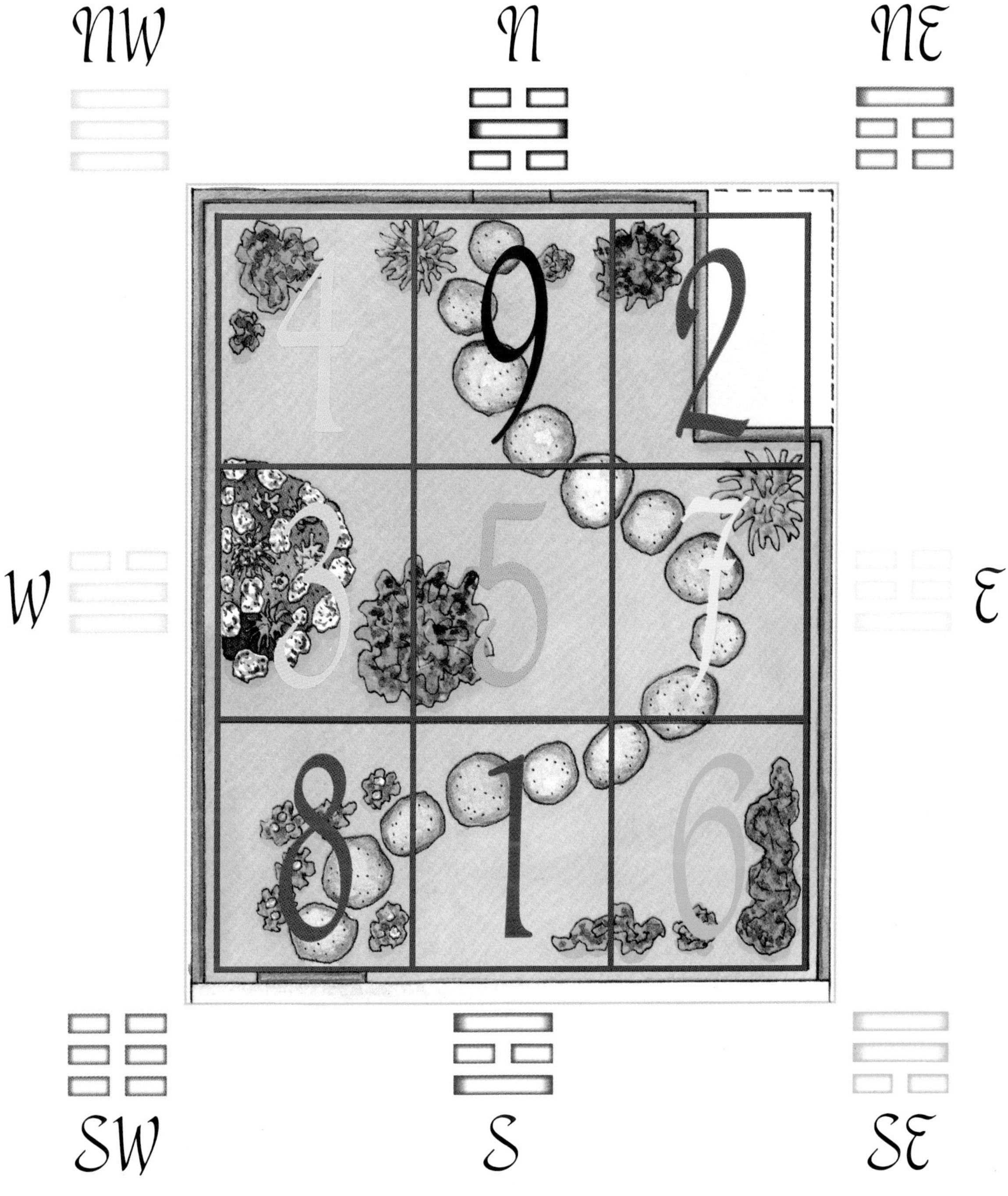
NW
N
NE
4
9
2
3
5
7
8
1
6
W
E
SW
S
SE

The Eight Enrichments Method

T his system is the easier of the two since it does not involve doing any more work with a compass and ruler than you have done already. Beginning with the rule that we start at the direction the garden faces (or the entrance or back door if a facing direction is not obvious) we allocate another set of meanings to the trigrams. These are:

1. Fame

2. Health and peace

3. Pleasure and indulgence

4. Friends and new beginnings

5. Relationships

6. Children and family

7. Wisdom and experience

8. Wealth

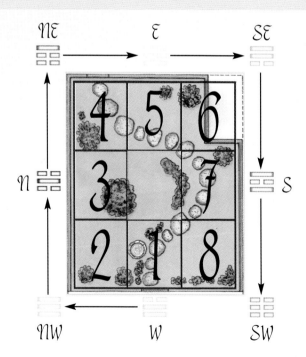

So, if we return to our first example garden which faces West, the direction of the White Tiger and the trigram Tui we find that this sector now also refers to one's fame and reputation. Consequently as we progress clockwise around the garden, one's health is symbolised in the sector of the trigram Ch'ien and one's pleasures in the area of K'an as follows:

1. **Fame is found in the West and the trigram Tui.**

2. **Health and peace are found in the Northwest and the trigram Ch'ien.**

3. **Pleasure and indulgence are found in the North and the trigram K'an.**

4. **Friends and new beginnings are found in the Northeast and trigram Ken.**

5. **Relationships are found in the East and the trigram Chen.**

6. **Children and family are found in the Southeast and the trigram Sun.**

7. **Wisdom and experience are found in the South and the trigram Li.**

8. **Wealth is found in the Southwest and the trigram K'un.**

In short, the trigrams have not changed position. They are still aligned with their respective compass directions. However, the meanings of the areas as they relate to you have changed somewhat from those described in the Lo Shu Magic Square Method. Even so, these two sets of meaning need not be contradictory and by fulfiling the conditions of good Feng Shui in one system you will be automatically fulfiling them in the other.

Now connect the directions of the trigrams in your garden to the meanings of the sectors in the Eight Enrichments Method.

The Shape of Your Garden

Jts may seem superfluous to point it out but the overall shape of your garden is of first importance when assessing the general Feng Shui of the area.

When you have decided on whether to use the Lo Shu Magic Square Method or the Eight Enrichments Method to divide up your space the next thing to consider is whether any of the segments are missing, enlarged or simply messy. For instance, if you have decided to use the Eight Enrichments to divide your garden, it is conceivable that one or more of the segments is completely absent or stunted by the very shape of your property. If this is the case, fear not because there are some simple Feng Shui "cures" that can be applied to the problem (p.57).

All this talk of garden shape is all well and good but we also have to think about how many gardens and open spaces actually surround your home.

How many gardens are there ?

In most cases this will be a simple question to answer. If you live in a terraced property the garden or yard will usually be at the back of the house. The house itself will provide one of the boundaries, the back door usually being the facing direction. However if you have a property with a front and back garden do you count all of your property including the house in your overall Feng Shui design, or treat each garden as a separate entity?

In classical Feng Shui, the whole of the property is considered as one, but this is not always easy when you consider that Western architectural design came into being without the benefit of oriental wisdom. Even so there are many detached properties that can be assessed in this way. Of course even if you do regard your house as part of the overall Feng Shui of your property, the interior Feng Shui will retain its importance, but to ensure that the Chi that enters your home is positive, the exterior must also be harmonious.

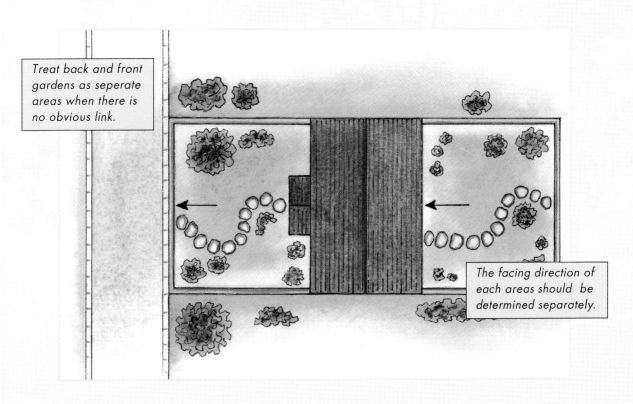

Treat back and front gardens as seperate areas when there is no obvious link.

The facing direction of each areas should be determined separately.

However, if you are in possession of a building that has both front and back gardens which do not connect except through the house or via a small alleyway it is probably best to apply Feng Shui to each of them as distinct areas. In itself this approach does present a minor problem. After all if you own a back garden surrounded by walls with no obvious facing direction save the back door, the same

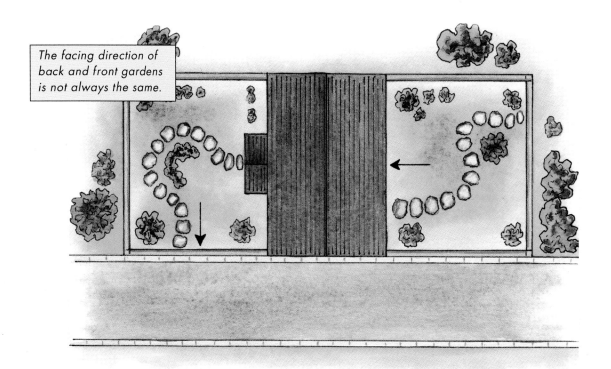

obviously does not apply to the space at the front of your house. Here the facing

direction will tend to point away from the house, usually towards the street so in the

case of both front and rear gardens the facing direction will tend to be, but not

necessarily be the same.

The facing direction of
back and front gardens
is not always the same.

Awkward gardens

Its is unlikely that your garden, or indeed anyone else's will be exactly square. A

corner or two may be absent. This may be an indication that means that some aspect

of your life is blighted in some way. For instance, in the Lo Shu system the Wealth

Area (the far left corner from the back door) may be missing and this will usually mean that either money is a problematic factor in your life or that you will be in debt. Likewise a small or absent Fame area will result in a diminishment of your reputation. Conversely, any enlarged sector will significantly enhance the Lo Shu sector or one of the Eight Enrichments often to the point that the associated area (Wealth, Fame, Relationship etc) of your life will be too busy and take up a disproportionate amount of your time and attention.

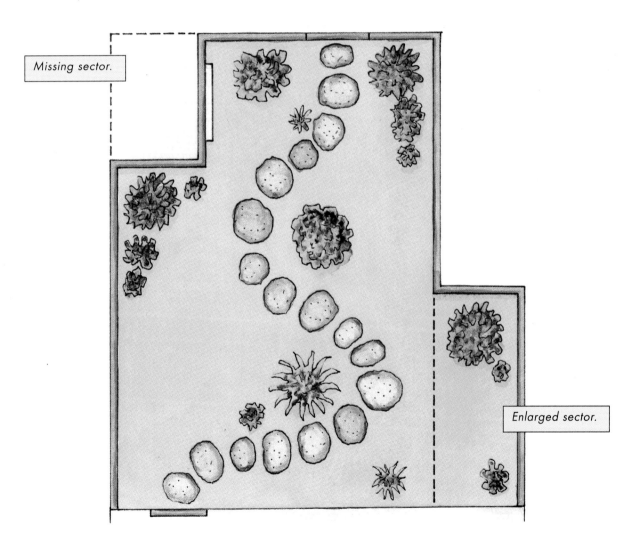

Missing sector.

Enlarged sector.

If the problem is one of a missing sector with clear-cut angles, then the lack of this area can be remedied by the use of a mirror, much as one would be used in interior Feng Shui. Correctly placed the mirror will create an illusion of space where in actuality none exists.

A correctly placed mirror will help to remedy the problem of a missing sector.

On the other hand, an overly large sector may make your life too busy and time consuming. You may find that the area of life that the sector symbolises causes you to be too obsessive and neglectful of other concerns. It is a general rule that complexity in an enlarged sector will directly correlate to complexity in the associated area of your life. If this is a problem then Feng Shui has a cure for this too. This area of the garden must be cleared of clutter. It should be kept as simple as possible, even to leave it clear of all distinguishing features if at all possible. It is certainly not a good idea to fill it with plants, ornaments or garden furniture. Even if this happens to be in a Water or Metal area, it would not be beneficial to place a water feature here because this will only serve to add to the already over-charged Chi flowing from the problem into your life.

Simple Feng Shui Cures

There are eight simple remedies that will cover most of the problems to be found in a normal garden. According to tradition each of these cures is associated with a particular direction and its governing Element, but in practice they tend to overlap in effect and can be used in any part of the garden where there is a problem. All you have to do is work out which one is appropriate in your space.

The simple cures are:

Light

Life

Movement

Stillness

Straight Lines

Sound

Colour

Devices

Although this Feng Shui cure can be used anywhere it is needed in the garden it is particularly suited to the South part of your property because light itself is associated with the Fire Element. The use of light as a Feng Shui remedy is self-explanatory. Good garden Feng Shui involves a balance between the Yang of light and the Yin of shade. So if any sector of your garden is too dark because of an overhanging tree or other darkening factor then the cure is to add some light by cutting back the overhang, or undergrowth to allow light to flood in. If this is not a sufficient solution you could turn the problem around by hanging some attractive lanterns from the overhanging branches. If this does not appeal then you could consider the addition of electric lighting to this area or go for the more natural solution of introducing plants which are "fiery" in nature or have foliage with is reflective of light such as eucalyptus or artemisia. You may even consider painting an adjoining wall a bright orange or red to increase definition in this area.

If a sector is too dark due to overhanging trees, cut them back to allow light to flood in.

The addition of bright fiery coloured flowers and foliage will help remedy dark areas.

If all else fails add a few attractive lanterns or even electric lighting to problem dark areas.

Life

It is a basic Feng Shui principle that anything living creates Yang energy so it follows that if there is an area of your garden which is sterile such as a concrete patio the encouragement of living creatures in this area would be beneficial. The encouragement of life can be as simple a matter as the addition of a bird-feeder but also includes plant pots with luxuriant foliage, planting flower-beds, especially those which include lavender, honeysuckle or other strongly scented plants which bees and other insects love. If, however the problem

Encourage wild life to enter an area by putting up a bird feeder or nesting box.

exists in a sector which is compatible to the Water Element the inclusion of a pond or a bird- bath to bring living things to this area. There is another point to consider. Since children burn off more Yang energy than anyone else, think about creating a play area here because nothing enhances life more thoroughly than excited children. The "life" cure is particularly suited to the Northern part of the garden but in practice can be used anywhere where the energy is slow moving or stagnant.

Add a pond to a sector which is compatible to the Water Element.

Movement

This is another Feng Shui cure that is self-explanatory. Any movement is said to encourage the flow of Chi. In areas where the energy is stagnant the beneficial effects of Chi can be encouraged by the use of mobile objects or plants that move in the wind. Ornamental grasses such as pampas grass are ideal for this purpose. If this solution is not practical then the perennial Feng Shui favourite the wind-chime (preferably made of a material that is compatible with the prevailing Element of the segment in question). Another traditional solution is the use of flags to flap in the breeze. Again, if the Element of the garden segment is conducive to use of the Water Element, then an active water feature, a fountain or a bubbling stream would be the ideal Feng Shui cure for a stagnant area. The Northern direction would be the preferred direction for a water feature such as this.

Wind-chimes are a simple and easy way to create movement.

Ornamental grasses are ideal for creating movement in an area to encourage the flow of Chi.

As you might imagine the Stillness cure is used in areas of the garden where the energy is too strong. Anything that moves would only serve to increase the strength of the positive Chi and make that segment unstable and difficult to cope with. This cure is associated with the West where the fierce energy of the White Tiger enters the garden. In many ways, an over active part of the garden acts like an enlarged

A still pond will help to calm the wild Chi entering from the West.

portion of your property and the same cure tends to apply. Bear in mind that each portion of the garden does represent a part of your life. It won't matter if you prefer to use the Lo Shu Magic Square divisions or the Eight Enrichments Method the result will be the same. Constant dramas that cause you to pay too much obsessive attention to

your cause of distress at the expense of other important issues. The recommended Feng Shui cure is to place a large immobile object in this sector to counteract the Yang energy. Remember that Yin is associated with heaviness. A statue, a boulder or a heavy pot would do but traditional thinking suggests a still pond to calm the wild Chi.

Large immobile objects are an easy cure when stillness is required.

Although straight lines tend to be frowned on in Feng Shui and considered conduits for Sha Chi or "Secret Arrows" they do have their use in the garden. Their major use is when there is one over-actively Yang area and a segment that is too passively Yin. The theory goes that by connecting the two with a straight path you will leech away some of the Yang into the Yin thus curing both areas at once. Of course Feng Shui is extremely adaptable so a path is not a necessary ingredient for the cure. You may prefer to use a straight jet of water, some plants such as bamboo which tend to be pretty vertical or a long, low garden seat between the two segments to make the connection. Even beanpoles and trellises can be used to connect two troublesome areas. This cure is especially effective in the South-west segment of the garden.

Trellises are ideal for connecting two troublesome areas.

Straight plants such as bamboo are good for balancing out Yang and Yin areas.

Straight pathways linking the two troublesome areas will help cure the problem.

Sound

This Feng Shui remedy is best utilised in the North-west segment of the garden. Here, the introduction of plants or objects that make a sound is an excellent way of introducing beneficial Chi energy into an area that is too dark or stagnant. Obviously wind-chimes again make an appearance here as do plants which rustle, the sounds of a rippling brook or a fountain. Insects and birds too create Chi both by their life force and the sounds that they make so a flower bed to attract bees or the addition of a bird table not only enhance the

The sound of flowing water is ideal for encouraging beneficial Chi.

"Life" cure but also the "Sound" remedy. A play area for children will also inevitably create noise. Hopefully sounds of happy laughter rather than tears will be the result.

Plants that rustle in the breeze introduce beneficial Chi into problem areas.

Use wind-chimes to create sound in dark stagnant areas.

The use of colour in any segment of the garden is very much a matter of personal taste as well as good Feng Shui. Colour can be used to enhance Yang energy with bright vibrant tones, or to promote Yin with

Bright vibrant tones promote Yin energy in an area.

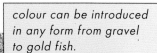

A dab or two of paint will enhance a drab area.

pastel shades and darker hues. The colour cure is most effective when one uses flowers to enhance an area of the garden, but a judicious dab or two of paint can be equally as potent. Colour cures are usually necessary when dealing with a small, drab backyard so that even in winter the vibrancy of life is still evident in your personal space. Though this remedy is ideally suited to the North-east there is no limit to the amount of

colour can be introduced in any form from gravel to gold fish.

colour one can employ in all other areas. Colour may be used in many imaginative ways, tiles or interesting gravel can be utilised in an Earth area, goldfish can be placed in a pond in a Water segment while, red ribbons can be utilised the Fiery South and so on. The limit lies only with boundaries of your imagination.

This is probably the strangest of the eight Feng Shui cures for the garden simply because it employs the common lawnmower, strimmer, scythe, barbecue, compost heap or even a humble broom. In short anything that has a practical function in or out of the garden. I have seen a particularly interesting and pleasing arrangement utilising a rusty old clothes mangle in the Earth area of a friend's garden. The theory behind this goes that the energy inherent in the

Even a simple broom can communicate its energy to the environment.

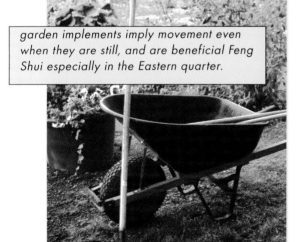

garden implements imply movement even when they are still, and are beneficial Feng Shui especially in the Eastern quarter.

use of any device is communicated to its immediate environment. So, in a spiritual sense a broom has the potential of brushing, therefore it always brushes. Devices imply movement even when they are not actually moving. This is considered to be good Feng Shui especially in the Eastern quarter.

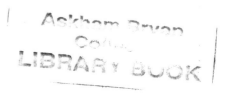

The Garden Entrance

Y et again we return to the concept of direction with a few traditional tips on how to best cope with the various types of Chi associated with the four symbolic animals. If you enter your garden via a gate this should be welcoming with a winding path leading from the entrance to your house. As usual in Feng Shui a curved gate will be preferable to one that is made up of straight lines. A solid gate will tend to prevent Chi from entering the garden so one when it is opened the stagnant Chi that has waited outside so to speak will rush in like a torrent and harm the family fortunes. Similarly, a curved path leading away from the entrance is infinitely preferable to a straight one. Positive Chi likes to meander gently and a straight line from the gate will increase its speed with unfortunate results. The same applies to larger gardens, paths and drives.

A South facing entrance

An arched gate that is tall and open is the
recommended entrance type for the Southerly
direction. The fiery Chi from the direction of the
Red Bird needs to be slowed to achieve the
maximum benefits from this exuberant Yang energy.
Even if you do not have a gate of full height, try to
incorporate an arch in the design of the entrance.
Another option would be to plant trees on either
side of the gate to provide a touch of Yin shade to

mellow this brightest of Chi
forces. However if the areas to
the South is open you will suffer
from too much Yang in your
garden so you will have to
increase the height of the
boundary preferably with tall
bushes or trees to provide more
shade to offset the overly
powerful Yang Chi.

A West facing entrance

Since the West is the direction of the fierce White Tiger, Chi from this direction should not be encouraged (Unless of course you have a North facing garden which would benefit from a shot of Tiger energy). A gate in the West should be solid and incorporate some metal in its construction. It need not be a complete door yet it should have a sense of stability about it. Another tip for a West facing gate is to interrupt the flow

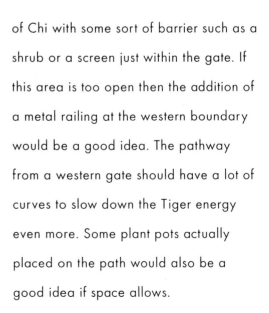

of Chi with some sort of barrier such as a shrub or a screen just within the gate. If this area is too open then the addition of a metal railing at the western boundary would be a good idea. The pathway from a western gate should have a lot of curves to slow down the Tiger energy even more. Some plant pots actually placed on the path would also be a good idea if space allows.

A North facing entrance

The Chi from the direction of the Black Turtle is rather lazy and slow so to benefit from its positive effects a large expansive entrance is recommended. If at all possible it is probably best to do without a gate in this direction, open space being more beneficial. There should be no obstacles to the passage of Chi, and even though the path should still meander it should be more angular than paths from other directions. The area around a northerly entrance should be kept clear to allow the

passage of as much Chi as possible. Another point to consider is that traditionally, a northern gate should not be close to the corner of your garden because the angle will tend to redirect the Chi away from your home. If the entrance is found here then it is recommended that you move it closer to the middle of your boundary.

The fertile Chi that originates in the direction of the Green Dragon is extremely beneficial. You can count yourself fortunate if your garden gate is in this direction. The Dragon energies should be encouraged by a wide entrance, a gateway made of wood which is the Element of the East. Of course, too much of a good thing can cause its own problems and your garden is in serious danger of becoming

overgrown and difficult to manage with an easterly entry-way. If you find that this is the case then a barrier of some sort just within the entrance would be a good idea to slow down this type of Chi. If your garden still resembles a tropical rain forest, then you'll have to utilise the Destruction Cycle to get rid of some of the excess Dragon Chi by ensuring that the obstacle is metal or at the very least symbolises that Element.

Backyards

If the only open space at your disposal is a backyard this is no bar to good Feng Shui even if the only use this space has is as a storage area for garbage. You can still create a harmonious environment in the smallest space by following a few simple guidelines. The rules of direction and Enrichments remain the same even in a small space though there will be little room to differentiate between them. So it becomes even more important to get the Feng Shui of the whole area right and then everything else will fall into place.

Good Feng Shui can still be practised even in a small backyard.

The first thing to do is have a good clean up. Lack of clutter is more important in a restricted space simply because any mess will be so noticeable. It is especially important to keep the central area of your yard clear because this sector governs the health of the family.

If you have high enclosing walls around your yard consider painting them a light colour to enhance the light and create an illusion of space.

Dustbins should be screened in some way so that they are not immediately visible from the back door of your home. A trellis with honeysuckle growing up it is a good idea especially as yards often trap smells. Honeysuckle and many other fragrant

It is important to clear away any clutter, especially in a small area.

Paint high enclosing walls a light colour to create an illusion of space.

Keep the centre of your backyard clear as this sector governs the health of the family.

A small water feature will enhance an enclosed area.

Fragrant plants disguise any unpleasant smell which may build up in a small backyard.

Small shrubs in pots will add height and greenery.

plants will ensure that the smells you trap will be pleasant ones. It would also be a good idea to arrange several heavily scented potted plants in front of your dustbins to both conceal their shape and odour. While on the subject of plants in pots, why not include some dwarf conifers in your design to add height and variety to the greenery.

A water feature is usual in a garden which has been designed the Feng Shui way. It doesn't matter if it is small as long as it fits in with the general layout of the space you have available. A bird bath, rainwater barrel or perhaps a series of pots with a small pump fitted could cause water to cascade from one to another in a pleasing fashion.

If your yard is completely paved over then treat it like a patio or a path and allow small flowers to grow between the slabs. If you have room, maybe a curved border or flowerbed would be possible.

Who knows, you could grow to love your backyard so much that you will want to spend more time in it. So include a seat in your design to create a private arbour of your very own.

Garden Furniture

or the placement of garden furniture such as seats, picnic tables and sun-loungers one must first think about the layout of your garden. Practicality is of first importance here and the furniture in question must be in a place where you can relax and let the cares of the world pass you by for a while.

The location of garden seating especially is an indicator of whether the Lo Shu Magic Square Method of garden alignments or the Eight Enrichments apply in your case. This is because you will tend to sit in an area that symbolises the sector of your life you are most comfortable in. A quick glance at the meanings of the Lo Shu Square (p.40) and the Eight Enrichments (p.50) should clear up this question.

The first consideration for any garden furniture is practicality.

Furniture should be placed in an area where you can relax and let the cares of the world pass you by.

The divisions of the garden can also be used to enhance your life in interesting ways. For instance if you want a place where you can meditate, to think deeply about life's questions then consider sitting in the area of Wisdom. You could enhance your relationship be a placing a love-seat in the are of Relationships and if you really want to impress your guests then arrange some seating in your area of Fame or Wealth.

If you want a place where you can meditate and think deeply, place your furniture in the area of wisdom.

As with interior Feng Shui, your seating arrangements should be inviting and comfortable. Curves are, as usual preferable to straight lines except where a "Straight Line" cure is required (p.62) to join two troublesome areas together. You should have a view over most of your garden from your sitting position and this rule should apply even when you possess more than one external seating area.

Most garden seats are constructed of stone, wood, metal or plastic. The general Feng Shui rule about not using man made materials wherever possible also applies to garden furniture. The elemental sector in which the seat is to be placed should indicate which is the most suitable material for the furniture. Wood would be placed in the East, Metal in the West and North, stone in the South, south-east, north-east and centre. Of course even if you do have garden furniture that is not of the appropriate material for its placement, you can always paint it an applicable elemental colour to ensure harmony.

You should have a view of your garden from wherever you place your seating.

Try not to use man made materials for garden furniture.

The elemental sector should be compatible with the material your furniture is constructed of.

All garden furniture should look inviting and be comfortable.

Water Features

Water is very important in Feng Shui (Shui literally means water) and no traditional oriental garden is without one. It is said that positive Chi is attracted to water and of course an active feature such as a fountain or stream will create even more of the positive energy. However stagnant or dirty water is more likely to encourage the negative Sha Chi so make sure that you clean your pool, pond, fountain, stream or bird bath regularly.

Water also makes a useful alternative to the most of the simple Feng Shui cures. It can be used in any area of the garden including the sector governed by Fire as long as care is taken that there is a wooden feature close by (Water douses Fire, Fire feeds Wood).

Even if you dig a pond, you should endeavour to make it look as natural as possible with stones, pebbles and gravel. If you just use artificial materials such as fibreglass and plastics then make sure that these are concealed from all angles by more natural substances. Feng Shui is about living in harmony with nature so the more convincing your pond you will receive better results in terms of luck, happiness and health.

Positive Chi is attracted to water.

An active water feature such as a stream or fountain will create even more positive energy.

Ponds should look as natural as possible and be in harmony with nature.

A water feature is particularly beneficial in the western sector of the garden. The unruly energies of the metallic White Tiger will be calmed by the gentle sound of a rippling stream or bubbling fountain. However if the garden faces West then a still water feature such as a bird-bath might be best to calm the savage beast even more.

A still water feature is beneficial in the West to calm the White Tiger.

The gentle sound of a bubbling fountain also has a calming effect.

Natural or artificial streams, though producing positive Chi do present certain problems. For instance a stream which meanders through the garden may actually divide it in Feng Shui terms into two or more separate areas. The solution to this problem is simple, use plenty of bridges to cross the water. These need not be elaborate like the elegantly curving bridges of oriental tradition but they do need to be well secured at both ends. In most cases a simple stone slab or sturdy plank will do the job perfectly.

Bridges should be used to join any areas which have been divided by a stream.

To chose which type of water feature is ideal for your garden we must consider the facing direction once again. If the facing direction is Yang such as the South then plenty of Chi is already flowing into your garden so perhaps a small fountain or even a still pond would be best to calm the Chi down a little. If the Yin Chi of the North is the main influence then a strongly active water feature is recommended.

As a final point we should remember that with any water feature safety is an important consideration. Electrical supplies to power fountains and waterfalls should professionally fitted. Deep ponds should be avoided if you have small children, and heavy objects such as bird-baths should be securely fixed to ensure that a child cannot pull them over.

Safety is an important consideration. Electric supplies to fountains and waterfalls should be professionally fitted.

Use pebbles, stones and gravel as well as flowers and foliage to disguise any artificial materials.

Deep ponds should be avoided if you have small children.

Ornamental features and heavy objects should be fixed securely.

Pathways

It is a general rule of Feng Shui that a curve is preferable to a straight line unless there are exceptional circumstances such as a Northerly garden entrance. Therefore paths within a garden should meander gently from one area to another. However if you are stuck with a straight path of concrete, brick or paving stones the negative effect can be softened by the use of plants which creep over the edges to conceal the sharp angle. If you can manage to blur the harsh definition of the edges of a straight path you will prevent harmful Sha Chi from surging through your garden. You might consider allowing grass or small flowers such as pinks or saxifrage to grow through cracks or between the bricks or paving slabs to break up the harsh effect. If space allows placing potted plants along the path will also serve to soften the line.

Blur the edges of paving slabs by allowing plants to creep over the sides.

A curved path is preferable to a straight one.

Plants growing over the edges of a path will soften the line and help prevent the harmful Sha Chi from surging through your garden.

Paths should meander gently from one area to another.

Bedding Plants, Beds and Borders

The rules that apply to paths also have a bearing on borders and flower-beds. Again the Feng Shui maxim that a curved line is preferable to a straight one comes into play, to the point that it is better to have an overgrown border that blurs the definition of the line than have a neat one in its own little box so to speak. With larger flower-beds, a gentle series of curves along the edges will have a beneficial Feng Shui effect causing the Chi within the garden to meander.

In a vegetable garden the Feng Shui distaste for straight lines and long, narrow shapes can be something of a problem since many varieties of home grown produce are set out in parallel rows. Of course this arrangement will tend to create "secret arrows" which will be particularly troublesome if they are directed towards the home. The solution to this problem is to lay out your vegetable beds in short straight lines which vary in direction like a herringbone pattern. You might also consider a circular bed with vegetables radiating out from a large stone or other heavy feature in the centre.

In large borders a series of curves along the edge is beneficial.

Include some tall plants in your borders to provide some shade, movement and sound.

Flower or vegetable beds that are enclosed by a lawn or patio should ideally be circular, oval or octagonal in shape. It would also be a good idea to include some tall plants in your arrangement to provide some shade, movement and sound to this area of the garden.

It is better to have an overgrown border that blurs the definition of the line than a neat one.

Wide Open Spaces

ny wide unoccupied space within a garden tends to become either a lawn, patio or covered in gravel. However there is no difference in how these areas are treated in Feng Shui terms, except in the fact that grass is living while, concrete, brick or stones are dead. The general rule is that according to the principles of Yang and Yin any area that is open space needs to have an equivalent area taken up by smaller spaces such as flower beds, ponds, rockeries and other features which provide interest. It may be that your lawn or patio occupies ten square metres. In that

An open space needs to be balanced with equivalent areas of interest.

A "bare" area should not occupy more than half of the land available.

case you will need ten square metres dotted about your property to be reserved for bedding plants, shrubs, trees and of course the water feature without which a Feng Shui garden is not complete. Each of these features may take no more than lets say two square metres each in which case you will need five of them.

However if you only have a small garden a sense of proportion is important. Remember that any lawn, patio or other "bare" area should not occupy more than half of the land available.

A grassy area dotted with small flowers or moss is preferable to a manicured lawn.

The living grass of a lawn is a generator of Chi in its own right, yet that Chi does not tend to move without a little help. If you aren't too much of a perfectionist a

If your lawn is extensive, add interest by placing an attractive object in the space.

grassy area dotted with small flowers or with a little moss is preferable to the manicured "cricket pitch" effect of the more traditional western lawn.

If your lawn is extensive, then an attractive object in the centre of the space would add interest. Remember to take note of the direction of the lawn to pick something of a suitable material. A large stone in the Earth area, perhaps a wooden pergola in the East and so on.

In contrast to the Chi producing lawn, a patio creates nothing. Of course a paved patio need not be without life. You can distribute potted plants on its surface area, perhaps take up a flagstone or two and plant a small flower bed there, or to be truly traditional, encourage small plants to grow between the cracks to break up the harshness of a such a sterile area of the garden; herbs are excellent for this purpose as they give off a wonderful aroma when trodden on. The worst case scenario is a large slab of concrete that prevents life from flourishing in that area. If you do have an open area which has had concrete poured over it then special care must be taken to increase the Chi in that segment (see Simple Cures p.57).

Encourage small plants or herbs to grow between the cracks on patio pavers.

Potted plants on patios are good for breaking up the harshness of the area.

Create a curved path to your door using potted plants which will encourage positive Chi.

If the entrance to the garden from the house opens onto a patio this can prevent Chi from entering the dwelling. This problem can be solved by creating some sort of path to the door. A few potted plants arranged on either side of the door and extending in a gentle curve would create interest and encourage positive Chi. Again the worse scenario involves and expanse of concrete especially if this is cut off by a straight line causing a step down to the lawn. In this case, visually breaking up the harsh line is of primary importance so treat yourself to some flowering shrubs in pots to disguise the problem. If the facing direction is compatible to the Element Wood, then some simple decking laid out in a herringbone pattern would help to enliven your patio.

Ornamental Features

The use of statues, urns and attractive stones and logs come under this heading. Ideally, if a statue is used to further beautify an area of the garden it should be suggestive of some of the symbolic associations of that area. The correspondences of the Eight Trigrams such as the symbolic animals or a perhaps

use ornamental features to further beautify an area of the garden.

a theme suggested by the individual Trigram's meaning would be a good idea. However, the theme does not have to be oriental in style or subject matter. After all, garden centres usually have a selection of classical figures that can easily be tied into the Feng Shui Elements and directions. You may consider a statue of a dolphin for the northern quarter to symbolise Water, or an amply endowed stone lady for the Southwest the area of K'un. The possibilities are endless so use your imagination.

Urns are good and can be adapted to several of the simple cures.

Natural materials are preferable to man made.

Glazed urns can be used to good effect because they can be adapted to several of the Simple Cures (see p.57). Natural materials are of course preferred and care should be taken that anything placed in the garden is elementally compatible with its direction.

If you use attractive stones that have been found in the countryside or on a beach then you must take care that they do not resemble any living thing too closely. A stone with a funny face might be amusing but if that face expresses anger or other negative emotion it should be turned away from the dwelling otherwise it will symbolically project that emotion into family life. Objects have the appearance of having yawning mouths are particularly to be avoided because tradition states that these mouths will gulp down the family fortunes.

Index

Index